PREVENTION GROUPS

Other Books in the Prevention Practice Kit

Program Development and Evaluation in Prevention (9781452258010)

Prevention and Consultation (9781452257990)

Prevention in Psychology (9781452257952)

Social Justice and Culturally Relevant Prevention (9781452257969)

Public Policy and Mental Health (9781452258027)

Evidence-Based Prevention (9781452258003)

Best Practices in Prevention (9781452257976)

To my loving husband, Bill, for his never-ending support and encouragement.

PREVENTION GROUPS

ELAINE CLANTON HARPINE
University of South Carolina

Los Angeles | London | New Delhi
Singapore | Washington DC

Los Angeles | London | New Delhi
Singapore | Washington DC

FOR INFORMATION:

SAGE Publications, Inc.
2455 Teller Road
Thousand Oaks, California 91320
E-mail: order@sagepub.com

SAGE Publications Ltd.
1 Oliver's Yard
55 City Road
London EC1Y 1SP
United Kingdom

SAGE Publications India Pvt. Ltd.
B 1/I 1 Mohan Cooperative Industrial Area
Mathura Road, New Delhi 110 044
India

SAGE Publications Asia-Pacific Pte. Ltd.
3 Church Street
#10-04 Samsung Hub
Singapore 049483

Acquisitions Editor: Kassie Graves
Editorial Assistant: Elizabeth Luizzi
Production Editor: Brittany Bauhaus
Copy Editor: QuADS Prepress (P) Ltd.
Typesetter: C&M Digitals (P) Ltd.
Proofreader: Jeff Bryant
Indexer: Diggs Publication Services, Inc.
Cover Designer: Glenn Vogel
Marketing Manager: Lisa Sheldon Brown
Permissions Editor: Adele Hutchinson

Library of Congress Cataloging-in-Publication Data

Prevention groups / editors, Elaine Clanton Harpine.

p. cm. — (Prevention practice kit)
Includes bibliographical references and index.

ISBN 978-1-4522-5798-3 (pbk.)

1. Group counseling. 2. Group problem solving. 3. Preventive health services. I. Harpine, Elaine Clanton, 1952-

BF637.C6P74 2013
158.3'5—dc23   2012040372

12 13 14 15 16 10 9 8 7 6 5 4 3 2 1

Brief Contents _____

Detailed Contents _____

Acknowledgments_____

I wish to express my appreciation to Bob Conyne and Andy Horne for their help and support. A thank you also goes to all of the children, youth, university students, community volunteers, parents, teachers, and university faculty who I have had the pleasure of working with while developing group-centered prevention programs.

1

What Is a Prevention Group?

A *third grader diagnosed with autism by the school was enrolled in an after-school program because of academic failure and inability to work with others in the classroom. Academically, he could read above his grade level, when he could be persuaded to read at all. His spelling skills also rose above grade level, yet his level of cooperation in the classroom and his desire to learn were sporadic. One minute, he would sit down and work as the teacher requested; the next minute he would be running around the room, refusing to sit, grabbing other students' work from their desk, and refusing to try to read, write, or spell. The after-school program in which the student was enrolled emphasized learning how to work together in a cooperative classroom-style setting.*

Was this student enrolled in a prevention group?

A group of teenagers met once a week. Their goal was community service. First, they organized, wrote, and presented a play for their neighborhood about sharing and caring for others. Next, they worked to raise the money to help inner-city children who were struggling to learn English as a second language. The group met each week for over a year; group sessions always centered on serving others.

Were these teens participating in a prevention group?

Parents brought their young preschool children for dinner and group sessions at a local community center. Everyone ate a free dinner. After dinner, the preschool children went to a classroom arranged with toys and tables for their age level. The teacher talked with the children about how to follow rules and play cooperatively. Arguments and fights among the children occurred daily. The teacher taught how to resolve conflicts without fighting. While the children attended their classroom session, parents participated in interaction-focused parenting classes.

Would this community-based program be classified as a prevention group?

Newlyweds, both in their second marriage, attended a program about communication for married couples. The program gave couples a chance to practice decision-making skills, problem-solving strategies, and anger management.

Were these married couples involved in a prevention group?

The answer to each of these questions is yes. Prevention groups can be for any age-group and serve a variety of purposes. Prevention groups typically incorporate positive group interaction, using group skills to solve the problem for which the groups were organized. Prevention groups also seek to enhance skills and competencies so that participants can avoid dysfunctional behavior and problems in the future. A recent special journal issue about prevention groups outlined the following definition:

> Prevention groups utilize group process to the fullest extent: interaction, cohesion, group process and change. The purpose of prevention groups is to enhance members' strengths and competencies, while providing members with knowledge and skills to avoid harmful situations or mental health problems. Prevention groups occur as a stand-alone intervention or as a key part of a comprehensive prevention program. Prevention encompasses both wellness and risk reduction. Preventive groups may focus on the reduction in the occurrence of new cases of a problem, the duration and severity of incipient problems, or they may promote strengths and optimal human functioning. Prevention groups encompass many formats. They may function within a small group format or work with a classroom of thirty or forty. Prevention may also be community-wide with multiple group settings. Prevention groups use various group approaches. Psychoeducational groups are popular and, while some prevention psychologists work within a traditional counseling group, others use a group-centered intervention approach. Two key ingredients for all prevention groups are that they be directed toward averting problems and promoting positive mental health and well-being and that they highlight and harness group processes. (Conyne & Clanton Harpine, 2010, p. 194)

Let's look at this definition for a minute. If the newlyweds discussed in the example above had participated in a group that sat and listened to a dynamic motivational speaker each week, would their group have been classified as a prevention group? No, sitting and listening to a speaker, no matter how dynamic or inspiring the speaker may be, is not a prevention group. Sitting and listening is passive involvement and does not include group interaction. For our married couples to be involved in a prevention group, the married couples must interact together as a group. This book's key position is that for any prevention group to succeed, it must incorporate constructive group interaction and positive group cohesion while fully utilizing the therapeutic healing power of group process.

_____Prevention Groups Must Be Interactive

Interaction involves talking, sharing ideas, solving problems, and evaluating. Interaction is not passive. For a group to be interactive, each person in the group must be free to talk, share ideas, and work with others in the group. Interaction must be structured, directed, or facilitated toward an overall goal, which will lead to change and positive mental health and well-being. Many school-based psychoeducational prevention groups suffer from lack of interaction. All too often, teachers and school counselors use the psychoeducational format, using the desire to impart information as an excuse to lecture students. While psychoeducational prevention groups can provide an excellent prevention format, lecture in any guise is not _group_ prevention. A teenage program on drug abuse incorporating 40 minutes of lecture on the dangers of drug use and 20 minutes on role plays is neither interactive nor a prevention group.

Group Process Is the Key to _____Success in Group Prevention

Prevention groups must provide more than an opportunity to talk. Prevention groups must provide a cohesive atmosphere (Conyne, 2004). Cohesion entails cooperation, a warm supportive atmosphere, understanding, acceptance, and healing of old wounds; cohesion enables group members to change by helping group members form a bond, an attachment—a sense of belonging (Clanton Harpine, 2011). Having the bullies and the students being bullied sit down together to discuss their feelings in a school-based setting does not constitute a prevention group because simply expressing one's feelings does not necessarily guarantee cohesion. Students might explain how they feel about being bullied, their anger, and their fears, but that neither guarantees understanding or acceptance nor ensures that the discussion will lead to a sense of belonging. You may have a school that discusses the problem of bullying vigorously—school administration, teachers, even the student body, but if both sides—the bullies and those being bullied—do not form a bond of understanding and acceptance, any attempt at prevention will fail. Prevention groups must be cohesive, and they can only obtain this cohesion through group interaction. Such interaction does not automatically occur when group members are placed in a circle of chairs. Cohesion can only be developed through the healing power of group process (Yalom & Leszcz, 2005). Effective group process develops a positive, supportive atmosphere through which change can occur (Marmarosh, Holtz, & Schottenbauer, 2005).

The Past and the Future

Group prevention is a fairly new concept. Joseph Pratt, a Boston physician who developed a group for tuberculosis patients, is credited with organizing the first prevention group in the 1920s (Hage & Romano, 2010). His groups began with a "lecture" and ended with time for patients to share feelings and concerns (Hage & Romano, 2010). He found that his group sessions helped reduce depressive symptoms. After Pratt's experience, others began to follow his example. Prevention spread to the schools. Jesse B. Davis is credited with starting the first guidance programs in public schools (Hage & Romano, 2010). Davis stated that groups provide an ideal setting for students to learn moral development as well as to obtain an education (Davis, 1914). Edward Lazell (1921) expanded group prevention to patients diagnosed with serious mental disturbances.

The concept of prevention had been born, and it began to spread throughout group work. Alfred Adler incorporated prevention techniques into his work with families, and Rudolph Dreikurs used prevention groups in his treatment of alcoholics (Hage & Romano, 2010). In his work with hospitalized psychiatric patients, L. Cody Marsh (1931) found that feelings and experiences shared by patients during interactive group sessions contributed significantly to their recovery.

Prevention in the 1920s, 1930s, and 1940s moved away from a lecture–response format. Group interaction was beginning to be seen as a key element. Kurt Lewin extended the theoretical base of prevention groups by emphasizing the importance that group process plays in any group (Hage & Romano, 2010), while Carl Rogers led humanistic psychologists to incorporate life skills development into their efforts to promote health and well-being throughout the life span (Rogers, 1970). During the 1990s, the call for expanded training in prevention techniques and standards for prevention group research echoed throughout group prevention.

Today, almost every aspect of mental health includes group prevention. Hospitals rely on prevention groups for heart attack patients and HIV/AIDS life skills training for patients. Schools use prevention group techniques for antidrug campaigns, bullying prevention, anger management, and academic failure. Schools have become one of the central foci of group prevention. Most of the prevention groups conducted with children and teenagers are held during school time (Kulic, Horne, & Dagley, 2004) or during after-school hours by school-based community organizations (Wandersman & Florin, 2003). Prevention groups are also being used by nursing homes to help elderly seniors. Community organizations are developing preschool and parenting programs using prevention techniques. Businesses and organizations use prevention groups to help workers reduce stress, find jobs, and resolve conflicts. Prevention groups are also emerging as a key player in social justice (Hage & Romano, 2010).

Today, interaction is seen as the key element in effective group prevention (Conyne, 2004). Techniques for using the positive effects of group process are becoming stressed more prominently every day in group prevention (Clanton Harpine, Nitza, & Conyne, 2010). There is a call for the next generation of group prevention specialists to develop prevention programs that make full use of group process, constructive interaction, and positive group cohesion. Group prevention can become one of our chief interventions in psychology, but for group prevention to continue to grow and succeed, group prevention specialists must focus on group process.

Types of Prevention Groups

Psychoeducational groups have been the predominant format in group prevention. There are many excellent evidence-based psychoeducational group prevention programs. Unfortunately, many group leaders misuse the psychoeducational label by confusing the need to impart information with a call to lecture. Many prevention group leaders are calling for change (Kulic et al., 2004; Nation et al., 2003; Wandersman & Florin, 2003; Weissberg, Kumpfer, & Seligman, 2003).

Group-centered prevention is a relatively new prevention technique being used in schools and community organizations with children and teens (Clanton Harpine, 2008). Group-centered techniques emphasize using group process to the fullest extent. Interaction is essential. All information is imparted through group process. In Chapter 4, we will look at a case example of a group-centered prevention program and illustrate how group-centered programs turn group process into group prevention.

Prevention techniques may also be incorporated into a therapy group, such as a teenage suicide group. In such a group, therapy and prevention needs intermingle. In the end, however, group process is still the key for both prevention (Conyne, 2004) and therapy (Yalom & Leszcz, 2005).

One of the key elements is that preventive interventions help reduce problems, while they boost improvement. Let's look at an example. A public school developed a schoolwide antidrug prevention program. The school brought in police officers, drug abuse counselors, professional athletes, and reformed drug abusers. Every day for a week, the students attended an assembly and listened to a different speaker. The students then returned to class and drew posters telling others not to use drugs. Drug arrests and drug use throughout the school actually increased. The prevention program, although well intended, failed. Why? The students were involved in only a passive role. They sat and listened to a lecture. They drew pictures and posted the pictures around the school, but the students were not involved, did not interact, and never had a chance to bond. The school did not become more cohesive because of the program. The prevention program did not bring about a change for students. Therefore, we must be cautious; just because a program wears the prevention label does not mean it is a true prevention program.

2

Group Process Is the Heart and Soul of Any Prevention Group

G roup process and group dynamics are not synonymous. Group dynamics combines the personality, fears, prejudices, experiences, and problems that group members bring to the group. In essence, the dynamics of a group arise from the people who compose the group. In contrast, group process is what people do with the group. Group process involves the interaction between members, the cohesion that does or does not develop within your group, and the bond or sense of belonging that develops between and among group members. Group process also includes the techniques and interventions that the group leader or facilitator uses to bring about a warm, cohesive, supportive atmosphere. To have a successful prevention group, the dynamics of the group members must be molded into a constructive, positive, cohesive group structure. You cannot simply place bullies from the classroom in the same group with those whom they are bullying and expect positive prevention results. Group members must learn how to show that they care for one another, that they trust each other, and that they accept and understand the feelings and ideas of each group member. Such acceptance does not happen automatically. The techniques and interventions used by the group leader will determine a prevention group's success or failure. To succeed, group prevention must fully use group process (Conyne, 2004). Group process is the means through which cohesion develops. Cohesion is more than just liking someone; it arises from a relationship that involves trust, acceptance, and the free exchange of ideas and feelings (Yalom & Leszcz, 2005). All group members have the desire and need to feel accepted by others in the group (Hogg, Abrams, Otten, & Hinkle, 2004).

Cohesion Is Essential for Change

The cohesiveness of a group grows out of these feelings of acceptance and belonging (Baumeister & Leary, 1995). The main purpose of a prevention group is to bring about change and personal well-being. Cohesion is essential for change (Marmarosh et al., 2005). Cohesion is also the bond that holds a group together (Ogrodniczuk & Piper, 2003). Cohesion does not mean conformity. Everyone in a cohesive group should be free to express individual ideas. If group members simply conform to the dictates of a leader or a few outspoken members of a group, then the group is neither cohesive nor well functioning. Cohesion includes freedom. If group members do not feel free to express their feelings and ideas, you do not have a cohesive group. Freedom of expression does not include hurting other group members or going off to do whatever an individual wishes. Freedom of expression within a cohesive group means that I am free to express my feelings and ideas, not that I am free to verbally attack or belittle others.

There must be interaction in a group if cohesion is to develop (Holtz, 2004). The more group members are involved in genuine equal interaction, the more likely group cohesion is to occur, but simply sitting in a group and talking does not create cohesion. Cohesion grows when group members share their ideas, feelings, fears, and needs. For cohesion to develop, group members need to demonstrate acceptance, understanding, and a deep degree of caring for others in the group. If even one person is shunned or left out, you do not have a cohesive group. Cohesion must include every single group member. If group members are being ridiculed, teased, or coerced, you do not have cohesion. A cohesive atmosphere should allow group members to express opposing ideas and feelings, challenge and question group norms, and encourage honest but not hurtful communication (Posthuma, 2002).

Making Prevention Groups Interactive

The best way to generate interaction in a group is to create a warm, supportive atmosphere. Interaction begins the instant group members arrive. Whether that interaction is positive or negative depends on how you organize and initiate group activities. If you start with a lecture or explanation, you block interaction. Interaction does not occur in a group any time you stop to explain rules, impart information, or lecture. Interaction must involve all group members. Theater-style chairs in an auditorium, a noisy gymnasium, or chairs gathered around a table are not conducive to group cohesion and interaction. Tables block interaction; noisy gymnasiums make it hard for the group members to interact, and bolted-down theater-style chairs do not encourage group members to interact, but the emotional climate of a group is more critical to group interaction and cohesion than the physical room arrangement. Children, for example, can function in a noisy gymnasium in a hands-on program and be very cohesive and interactive; therefore, strive for a good group setting but know that it is what you do in the group that is more important than the group setting itself. A good group setting helps you get started, but a truly interactive group can work around room obstacles. Start with action, not explanation. The interventions that you use to initiate interaction in your prevention group will vary depending on the age of your group participants, purpose of your group, and goals you hope to achieve. If you are uncertain how to initiate group interaction, the case examples in Chapter 4 offer suggestions on ways to initiate interaction at the beginning of a prevention group or turn to more comprehensive training guides that give step-by-step procedures for generating group interaction (see Clanton Harpine, 2011).

Creating Change in a Prevention Group

To generate group cohesion, group leaders must develop an underlying structure that allows cohesion to grow in a group. Irvin Yalom describes this structure as the 11 therapeutic factors needed for therapy and change in psychotherapeutic groups (Yalom & Leszcz, 2005). The same 11 factors are needed in a prevention group for cohesion to develop (Clanton Harpine et al., 2010).

An example will help demonstrate these principles. An 11-year-old girl had been retained twice for failing grades in reading. She was enrolled in an after-school prevention program designed to alleviate reading failure. Eight months later, she was passing reading for the very first time in her school career. Let's examine her case step-by-step through the 11 factors of change.

Hope is essential in prevention: Without hope, there can be no change or personal growth. Each person, regardless of age or station in life, has a strong need to belong with others in a group (Baumeister & Leary, 1995). Members of a prevention group need to feel that they can improve and change or learn a new skill (Deci & Ryan, 1985). Our young student who failed reading each year in school felt as if she was a failure. She acted out and misbehaved in class, so she would not be called on to read because she didn't want the other students to know that she could not read. Through hands-on skill-building group-centered interventions, she learned to read. She once again had hope.

Universality is essential in a prevention group. Although everyone fears rejection, learning that others share similar feelings can reduce the fear of rejection or failure (Fuhriman & Burlingame, 1990). The student in our example found acceptance, particularly through cohesive group activities, and learned that she was not the only student having trouble. She became willing to try new learning tasks and new group behaviors as she worked alongside others who were also trying to learn new skills.

Imparting information is seen as one of the primary tasks of many prevention groups, but group leaders must make sure that prevention group interventions actively involve all group participants. The way a prevention group teaches or informs makes a difference in whether that group becomes interactive and cohesive (O'Brien Caughy, Murray Nettles, & O'Campo, 2008). In many instances, it also determines whether a prevention group will succeed. In our example, the after-school program used hands-on learning centers to impart information. The students traveled between learning centers reading to complete an assigned task and practicing the phonetic skills necessary for learning to read. Our young student learned the skills she needed to read but in a hands-on interactive group format.

Altruism is therapeutic and aids prevention. Giving to others helps group participants grow individually and as a cohesive group. Giving to others also helps group participants to shift from the role of receiver to the role of providing for others (Holmes & Kivlighan, 2000). Giving to others can be a strong motivator in group prevention and strengthens group cohesion. The young lady in our example learned that she was not the only student having trouble, and more important, she learned how to help another student.

The prevention group becomes a new *peer group* for participating group members. Yalom explains the therapy group as becoming a new family group for participants (Yalom & Leszcz, 2005). The group in our example began to solve problems as a group as they worked together to paint a puppet stage. Sharing ideas, taking turns, and having to consider the feelings of others helped to build a more cohesive group.

Social skills often become an intricate component of the information being taught in a prevention group. By working as a group to solve a problem or make a decision, group participants learn life skills that can be transferred to the real world (Finn, Gerber, & Boyd-Zaharias, 2005). When those skills are taught through interactive strategies, such interactive teaching can actually enhance group prevention. As the students in our example worked together to paint a puppet stage, they had to use problem-solving strategies in order to decide what to paint. They also had to make decisions that were for the betterment of the entire group instead of what one individual might want or think. Learning to make decisions as a group is a much stronger prevention strategy than simply telling group members that we must work together as a group or to cooperate with others. Some skills must be experienced.

Modeling can be an essential step in the prevention process, but modeling must be positive and correct to aid prevention. The enthusiasm of hardworking group members can motivate uncertain group members. Negative modeling of negative behavior is destructive to group process (Bandura, 1997). Our student became motivated to try new skills that she refused to even consider during tutoring by watching others move around the room working at the different learning centers.

Interpersonal learning can be positive or negative in a group setting. The prevention group can become a mirror through which group members can interpret others' perspectives, but reflections are only helpful in a group setting if the group is cohesive, accepting, and trusting of one another (Baumeister & Leary, 1995). Interpersonal learning can become a positive component of prevention or it can become a detriment. For interpersonal learning to be positive in a group, it must include positive supportive interaction for all group members and a strong cohesive accepting group atmosphere (Brigman & Webb, 2007). Our student in the after-school example began to trust and work with others when she discovered that they were not going to make fun of her for not being able to read.

Group cohesiveness is essential for every group but particularly for prevention groups. Group cohesiveness reinforces the individual need to belong and be accepted in a group (Marmarosh et al., 2005). The student in our example had experienced teasing in the classroom because of reading failure, but in the prevention group, she found many students working at different skill levels. Teasing was not allowed. Positive cooperation and acceptance were continually taught through stories, puppet plays, and group activities.

Catharsis in a group (relieving the stress and anxiety) is only possible when you have a very strong cohesive group atmosphere. Positive and supportive group interaction provides the perfect setting for catharsis (Ablon & Jones, 2002). Honesty is important in a group, but group members must feel a sense of acceptance and have a sense of trust that other group members will not hurt them emotionally. If group members are afraid to share their feelings and ideas in a group, you do not have cohesion or acceptance.

Yalom identifies the 11th element as *existential factors* (Yalom & Leszcz, 2005). In group prevention, this might best be described as responsibility. Every group member has a responsibility to act in a positive and supportive way toward other members of the group. A group cannot reach or maintain group cohesion until every member accepts this responsibility. In life and in the group, we are all responsible for our words and actions. This is particularly true in a group setting. Hostile, negative group behavior can be very detrimental to group prevention efforts. The after-school prevention program taught students to take responsibility for their words and their actions through the manner in which the students learned to work together as a group.

If you want successful group prevention, you must build these 11 factors into your prevention program. Without these 11 factors, you will not achieve cohesion. Without cohesion, you will not accomplish successful prevention.

Making Sure That a Group Is Both Interactive and Cohesive

The way in which you organize group sessions and the interventions that you use to generate group participation will determine whether your prevention group is interactive or not. The group atmosphere and climate that you create will determine whether your group becomes cohesive or not. The level of group interaction and degree of group cohesion will determine whether your group program is successful in preventing unwanted behaviors and bringing about personal wellness and change (Ablon & Jones, 2002). Interaction and cohesion are both essential for any prevention group to be effective.

3

Research Supporting Prevention Groups

Prevention groups have been the topic of numerous research studies. Many of these studies review and evaluate the effectiveness of prevention group programs (Biglan, Mrazek, Carnine, & Flay, 2003; Durlak & Wells, 1997; Greenberg, Domitrovich, & Bumbarger, 2001; Kazak et al., 2010; Kulic et al., 2004; Tobler & Stratton, 1997; Twenge & Campbell, 2002). This chapter's purpose is not to summarize these research studies but to focus on what is needed in group prevention research to strengthen the effectiveness of prevention programs.

There is a cry for evidence-based group prevention programs. Although striving for evidence-based programming is definitely a desirable goal, it is not enough. Mere use of an evidence-based labeled program does not ensure evidence-based results (McHugh & Barlow, 2010). Whenever a group leader reinterprets the intentions and design of an evidence-based program, the effectiveness of such an evidence-based program is compromised (Kratochwill, 2007). In other words, if you want evidence-based results from an evidence-based program, you must use the evidence-based program as it was written and designed to be used (Kazak et al., 2010). You cannot rewrite your version of an evidence-based program and then expect the evidence-based results of the original program because you are no longer using the original evidence-based program (McHugh, Murray, & Barlow, 2009). Instead, you are using your untested translation of an evidence-based program. It is not the same. If you reinterpret an evidence-based program, you must retest your reinterpretation to prove that your program provides the same evidence-based results as the original program (Kazak, 2008; Langley, Nadeen, Kataoka, Stein, & Jaycox, 2010; Riggs, Bohnert, Guzman, & Davidson, 2010).

So how do we ensure evidence-based prevention results from our evidence-based research programs? Some suggest stricter adherence to manualized programs (Kulic et al., 2004), but while that is a noble suggestion, the mere existence of manuals does not guarantee that a group leader will follow the manual. A manual will not insure that a person who buys an evidence-based program manual uses it as it was designed and intended. We, as psychologists, mental health practitioners, and group program designers, must offer a method that will allow well-intended groups to find success and truly offer effective prevention programs (Greenberg et al., 2003; Nation et al., 2003). We must find a way to ensure that evidence-based research finds its way into evidence-based programming.

Program Packets

One proposal is to provide ready-to-use program packets. A program packet is a ready-to-use version of a program. Everything is included in the packet, so the group leader can use an evidence-based program without reinterpretation or adaptation. Program packets are written and adapted by the researcher to fit a variety of group settings and needs, which means that basically the same evidence-based program is presented in ready-to-use form for a variety of settings and group situations.

The benefits of ready-to-use program packets are reduced preparation time for personnel conducting prevention programs, stronger adherence to program design and intended implementation, and consequently more effective group prevention programming through stronger adherence to research-based programs. Ready-to-use packets will enable programs to be used as intended and thereby empower users to reap the evidence-based benefits of an evidence-based program.

An example is the *Camp Sharigan Project*, a program that began in 2001 to work with inner-city, at-risk children. *Camp Sharigan* is a motivational group-centered prevention program that focuses on improving reading skills as a means of preventing depressive symptoms, at-risk behaviors, and other mental health concerns (Clanton Harpine, 2010). Six published program packets use the *Camp Sharigan* group-centered approach. These include three school-based 1-week group prevention programs, two after-school prevention programs, and one in-class prevention program. The overall approach is the same, but each ready-to-use program packet has been written and adapted for specific settings and group needs.

All of the *Camp Sharigan Project* programs integrate hands-on remedial teaching techniques and group counseling motivational techniques; therefore, the program combines both the educational needs and the counseling needs of at-risk children (Clanton Harpine, 2011). The six *Camp Sharigan Project* programs emphasize rebuilding self-efficacy by using intrinsic motivators (internal desire not rewards or prizes). The program packet is a ready-to-use hands-on booklet that provides step-by-step instructions for students and those directing the program. The packet includes game cards, stories, puppet plays; everything that is needed to run the program is included. The counselor or teacher does not have to interpret the program or create materials for the program. The packet is complete. Using a ready-to-use program packet ensures that both the hands-on at-risk teaching methods and the motivational group counseling techniques are used correctly because they are written into the workstation booklets.

Program packets are only one suggestion. What we need in group prevention is more research on providing evidence-based implementation of evidence-based prevention programs. Evidence-based implementation of evidence-based programs should become one of the major research efforts in group prevention.

4

Case Examples

Prevention groups can help any age group deal with any number of problems. Three examples demonstrate the variety and diversity in prevention programming. Our first example examines a psychoeducational prevention group program for married couples. Our second example looks at a group-centered prevention program for at-risk children. Our third example is about prevention in an outpatient psychotherapy group. The primary role of a psychoeducational group is to prevent a problem from occurring by educating participants on a particular topic (Kulic et al., 2004), a group-centered prevention group combines the educational and psychological needs of participants into one group program and stresses rebuilding self-efficacy (Clanton Harpine, 2008), and a psychotherapy group works to remediate a psychological or personality-related problem (Gazda, Ginter, & Horne, 2001).

Case Example 1

Our first example is from "Communication for Married Couples," a 6-week program sponsored by a local university. The program was open to the community. Couples paid a fee to the university and met once a week for 2 hours over 6 weeks. Most participants attended in couples, and there were typically no more than 12 couples per program. The program was advertised throughout the community and was even featured on a local early morning TV program.

The program's goal was to share information about communicating more effectively as a couple. The couples program was a psychoeducational prevention program because its primary purpose was to educate or provide information (Gazda et al., 2001). The participants found one large circle of chairs as they entered the college classroom. There were no tables, but the university-style student desks did provide a note-taking armrest pad.

Each person received an index card, and markers were passed around the circle. Participants printed their first name in the upper left-hand corner of the index card on the side of the card without lines. Only first names were used at first so that each person could become known as an individual first and then later as a couple. Next, the participants drew pictures in the center of each card to describe themselves. This was not to be a picture of how they looked physically, but how they viewed themselves emotionally. Some suggestions included the following: (a) maybe you see yourself as a single grain of salt stuffed into a salt shaker with millions of other grains of salt, (b) perhaps you feel like an electrical outlet with multiple plugs and connectors and extension cords going in all directions, (c) maybe you are a swan floating on a tranquil pond, or (d) you might see yourself as the rope being used in a tug-of-war. After having a few minutes to draw their pictures, participants were divided into pairs by matching the first letter of names: "Anyone whose name starts with an A, stand up." Matching continued until all participants had been paired with someone new that they did not know. Thus, instead of starting the program with a discussion or speaker-to-audience talk about what the 6-week program would entail, interaction started immediately.

Newly formed pairs were given 5 minutes to write on the back of their cards (a) one thing that they had in common with the person just met and (b) one thing that was totally different. All pairs were then told to write their last names in the card's lower right-hand corner. Couples whose last names differed were asked to put the spouse's last name in parentheses. Then, pairs were asked to join with another pair, which, if possible, did not include their spouses. Again, pairs (now foursomes) were asked to list similarities and differences on the back of their card. Next, couples were brought together into groups of eight, which for some groups included spouses. Again, time was allowed for group members (eight in each group) to discuss and list similarities and differences. Next, chairs were brought back to a full group circle. Participants then described why they felt that the picture in the center of their card described them at the present time. Participants were also encouraged to tell the group something they hoped to accomplish during the 6-week program or give a reason for participating. The group also discussed similarities and differences. Members were asked, "Did you meet anyone new with whom you had something in common?" The role of individuality was discussed. The question was put to the group: "Is it okay to be different?"

Couples were next asked to add at least three similarities and three differences on the back of their card for their spouse. Married couples worked together to discuss their similarities and differences. Couples received a second index card, so they could list on one side of the card everything that they liked about their marriage and on the reverse side list things they would like to change about their marriage. After having time to share, they reported back to the total group as a couple to tell one thing that they *both* really liked about their marriage and one thing that they *both* wanted to change. This marked the beginning of decision making and compromise as a couple. Group structure was beginning to grow. Acceptance was beginning to take root.

Couples were also encouraged to think of themselves as individuals first and then as couples through the introductory name tag exercise. Therefore, an important principle of the program was initiated from the very beginning: You are two individuals who come together as a couple. This principle would become even more important as the couples moved into learning problem-solving and decision-making skills. The idea was to initiate interaction from the very beginning and to help the participants start off thinking of everyone in the group as an individual with similarities and differences. The first two principles being taught in this group were (1) that couples comprise two individuals who have both similarities and differences and (2) that such similarities and differences are not so unlike the similarities and differences we have with others in a group. By intermingling group participants and sending couples out as individuals, this program also initiated two group principles: (1) Cohesion requires that each person be seen and accepted equally as an individual—not as a member of a couple—and (2) for positive, constructive cohesion to develop in a group, members must interact with every other member of the group. This is especially important in a couples' group. You do not want one member of the couple to speak for the couple; you want both members to participate fully. You cannot solve communication problems if one person just sits and listens, while the other person speaks for the couple and explains how they feel. This happens all too often in programs for couples.

By dividing group members into pairs, and then into small groups, finally bringing all participants back together as a total group, group members were more willing to disclose meaningful information than they would have been if group members had been asked to share individually with the total group at the very beginning. Pairs and small groups allow people to interact together in a less threatening atmosphere. Disclosure is easier after working with other group members.

Initiating interaction and setting the stage for the development of cohesion from the very beginning of a psychoeducational program is very important. Don't start with a lecture; don't explain what the program will or will not do; don't tell people what they will learn; and don't explain which principles are or are not important in effective communication between married couples. Instead, show them. Demonstrate the communication principles being taught through how you use group process and the way you organize and initiate interaction.

It is also important to keep sight of the program's original intent. The couples gathered for this program because they wanted to improve their communication skills in order to have a stronger, more satisfying marriage. Yes, as a group facilitator you must initiate group process and lay the groundwork for positive cohesion, but you must also not lose sight of the expectations that group members bring with them to the first group session. Otherwise, couples may not see the advantage of reflecting on individual similarities and differences. Always make time for married couples to work together as a couple.

Each of the six sessions in this prevention group continued to emphasize group process, interaction, and cohesion while teaching married couples to communicate more effectively. Other sessions focused on perspective taking, decision making, and problem solving. Each week, the couples brought real examples from their marriages that they wanted to work on, such as how to save money to buy a house, who would be the primary caregiver with the children, whose career was more important. Using real-world problems made decision-making and problem-solving techniques more applicable. The participants continued to work as a total group, in small groups, and as couples throughout the 6-week program.

This psychoeducational prevention program was prevention oriented because, following the principles from Chapter 1, the intent of the communication for married couples program was "to enhance members' strengths and competencies, while providing members with knowledge and skills to avoid harmful situations or mental health problems" (Conyne & Clanton Harpine, 2010, p. 194). A happier marriage is healthier and better for everyone involved. Married couples will learn more and be more apt to apply what they learn from the prevention program to their actual marriage through a group-focused psychoeducational program than they ever would by listening to a speech. The couples brought real problems to the group, worked on these problems, and left with step-by-step decision-making or problem-solving techniques.

Group process is one of the strongest and most effective means to teach and convey information. Let the information grow out of the sharing of ideas within the group. This is particularly true for psychoeducational programs used in school-based settings or hospital settings. Heart patients being taught how to prevent another heart attack need to know facts, but facts can be learned through exploration in a group setting. A psychoeducational prevention program should never resort to lecture. So if you find yourself standing in front of your group speaking to them at the start, middle, or any time throughout the prevention program so that you can impart information, you know that you're doing it the wrong way. Use group process. Let group process teach the skills that you want your group members to learn.

Case Example 2

Our second case example is taken from an after-school program for children from a low socioeconomic neighborhood. Most of the children participating in this free community-based program are struggling or, in many cases, failing in school. Many of the children have been retained in a grade or are in danger of being retained. The program offers free transportation to and from the community center, free dinner 4 days a week, recreational activities, and free tutoring through a mentoring program. The community-based program works directly with the schools to serve as a link between the troubled neighborhood and the classroom. Most of the children in the program are not only plagued with academic failure but also have behavioral issues. Many of the children see themselves as failures and foresee no prospect of ever completing high school.

For this case example, we will look at how a group-centered prevention format was used in this school-based community setting. Group-centered prevention is a new, different approach for group prevention. Psychoeducational prevention programs usually focus only on life skills or guidance issues, but many researchers believe that prevention interventions in schools will succeed only when they are linked to academic performance (Brigman & Webb, 2007; Greenberg et al., 2003; Nation et al., 2003). Group-centered prevention programs address the academic needs of students together with their counseling needs using group process as the instrument of change (Clanton Harpine, 2011). Combining learning and counseling into a single program can enable school-based practitioners to focus on cognitive, affective, and behavioral skill building within the same program.

For the past 10 years, I have been designing and testing group-centered prevention programs with at-risk students. Some of my work has been in inner-city neighborhoods, while other sites have been more suburban or rural in nature. For the case study purposes of this chapter, we will look at my *Camp Sharigan* program (Clanton Harpine, 2010). *Camp Sharigan* is a week-long motivational reading clinic that meets for 2 hours a day and uses a hands-on, summer camp theme. *Camp Sharigan* stresses group process, especially interaction, cohesion, and the 11 curative factors (Yalom & Leszcz, 2005) of group process to bring about change.

The community center itself was a dingy, worn-out, overcrowded building. *Camp Sharigan* was held in the meeting room, which actually was not a large room at all. Tables, chairs, a stage area for music groups, a marked-off office area, 30 at-risk first through third graders, and 10 university students were all to be squeezed into the meeting room space.

When the children arrived on the first day, tables and chairs had been pushed to the edge of the room, dingy, poorly lit walls had been covered with colorful painted wall hangings creating a summer camp scene with forest, waterfalls, a bold beautiful sunrise, a rainbow, lake, and a mountain. The children and workers sat on cushions on the floor to encourage easier movement around the room to 10 learning centers. The children began by sitting on the floor in front of a large red stop sign that read *Stop, Read a Book*. Interaction begins through an *action story* as soon as the children enter and are seated. Children were selected to come forward and help act out the story, but all children were reminded that each day would begin with a story, and so if someone was not an actor for the story today, there would be an opportunity to be chosen on one of the other days—thus, starting the program with a theme of equal participation. The first story has the make-believe camp mascot, *Sharigan*, going out in search of a friend. *Sharigan* is a snake, and naturally snakes are not liked. *Sharigan* has many problems making friends. The story includes all types of sounds that the children make as the story is being told. Each child actor responds with the appropriate sound when their word is read in the story. Such an activity enhances listening skills, attention-focusing skills, and group cooperation. It is also an excellent way to initiate interaction with a group of children in a group setting. It is a controlled activity but interactive. At the close of the story, each child receives a *treasure hunt map*. The clues on the map direct the children around the room to each learning center. The children are then sent off to find their first clue. Each learning center is labeled and the label is part of the clue on the map. The *treasure hunt maps* are simply a way to distribute 30 children around the room to the learning centers in a fun way. The *treasure hunt maps* also continually remix small groups as the children travel from learning center to learning center and interact in different groups. This is much better than trying to move the children around the room in small designated groups. No two children work or learn at the same pace—one will be bored, the other frustrated and unable to complete the task before time is called, and the group moves on. *Treasure hunt maps* enable children to work together in groups but also allow students to work at their own individual pace and, thereby, individualize instruction.

Mount Reading consisted of an inflatable double air mattress used as a center where children could practice spelling *tricky* words and then climb up on the mountain to rest and read a book. Even though the children had to practice spelling before climbing up on the mountain, they lined up for a turn at *Mount Reading*. Spelling was no longer a dreaded chore but a fun activity. Spelling scores also improved by the end of the week, so the emphasis was not on play but on learning in a fun, hands-on way.

Each session also taught phonics skills. *Sharigan's Snake Pit* was a favorite with the children as they crawled through the tunnel and built words through letter sounds. The *Snake Pit* emphasized a different phonetic sound every day. Composing a word one letter at a time encouraged the children to match letters to phonetic sounds and also to recognize *tricky* words that are not spelled the way they sound. Students from university classes worked as learning center helpers to offer one-on-one tutoring and assistance. The learning centers emphasized reading, writing, spelling, sight words, phonics, word games to build vocabulary, comprehension, and learning to work together as a positive cohesive group.

Children who habitually fought and argued about everything worked together to paint a puppet stage. The children were told that they could paint wherever they wanted on the cloth, as long as they made sure that every single student was included. The children had to work as a group to figure out how to divide their puppet stage cloth so that everyone would have a space to paint and how to pull all of the ideas together into one complete group painting. Everything had to be equal. All decisions had to be group decisions; no one was allowed to be the boss.

The friendship theme from the opening action story was continued throughout the week. While the children looked for ways to help *Sharigan* make friends, *Sharigan* invited the children to come and "share the love of reading." *Sharigan* tells the children why he loves to read through puppet plays that are used to close each daily session. The children make puppets and read as puppet characters for *Sharigan's* stories and adventures with his friends.

Camp Sharigan is a portable, hands-on group-centered reading clinic that combines one-on-one tutoring through the use of learning centers with group process and hands-on intrinsic learning. *Camp Sharigan* is designed to travel to different schools or community sites. The wall hangings initiate excitement the instant the children enter the room. The hands-on learning centers keep the enthusiasm going throughout the week. Intrinsic, not reward-based motivators are used so that children leave with a renewed interest in reading. One example of an intrinsic motivator is the *pop-up storybook*. Each child makes a construction paper pop-up storybook with a mountain cover that opens. The inside pages display a house that pops up, a pop-up bedroom with a desk for studying, and a pop-up living room where books are featured instead of a television. The children spend the week making their book and writing a story to go inside their book. On the last day, children stand and proudly read their story and show off their pop-up book as they unfold each page. This intrinsic project allows each child to express their individual personality in how they decorate their book and through the story they choose to write. A pop-up book generates pride, and I have had many children tell me several years later that they still have their pop-up book from *Camp Sharigan*.

Academically, *Camp Sharigan* focuses on reading. Reading is the primary academic emphasis because reading failure is so universal. The Nation's Report Card for 2009 estimated that 40% of all fourth-grade children cannot read at grade level and that 90% of students who drop out of school have been linked to early reading failure (National Assessment of Educational Progress, 2009). Brain imaging research has shown that intensive remedial reading programs can help change the "white matter" of the brain for children who are poor readers (Keller & Just, 2009). Reading failure is also linked to at-risk behaviors and mental health and well-being.

Discipline problems in the classroom, violence and aggression, bullying, delinquency, substance abuse and illegal drug use, crime and eventual prison incarceration, dropping out of school before graduation, and the development and tendencies toward depression and anxiety have all shown links with early reading failure (Catalano et al., 2003; Greenberg et al., 2001; Greene & Winters, 2006; Miller & Shinn, 2005; Nastasi, Moore, & Varjas, 2004; Orfield & Lee, 2005; Prilleltensky, Nelson, & Pierson, 2001; Snowden, 2005; Twenge & Campbell, 2002). Reading failure is more than just an academic problem; it is also a psychological problem. Research substantiates that children can improve both academically and psychologically through prevention programs (Nelson, Westhues, & MacLeod, 2003).

In recent research, students participating in the group-centered *Camp Sharigan* program improved significantly more than the control group, and follow-up testing 1 year later continued to show the *Camp Sharigan* students performing better (Clanton Harpine & Reid, 2009). *Camp Sharigan* has been used in schools (Clanton Harpine, 2005) and community-based organizations (Clanton Harpine, 2007).

Group-centered prevention programs take a different approach than psychoeducational prevention programs. Group-centered prevention programs stress teaching the necessary skills to help group participants change (Clanton Harpine, 2008). Skill building is more than just telling someone what they need to do or giving information; skill building requires that group participants be taught how to perform a skill correctly (Bandura, 1977). Group-centered prevention programs use group process to teach these skills.

Camp Sharigan became a key component of an overall comprehensive prevention effort at the community center. In this case, *Camp Sharigan* undertook to motivate at-risk children and increase their phonetic skills to rebuild self-efficacy and help these children return to the classroom ready to learn. As our definition in Chapter 1 stated,

> Prevention groups occur as a stand-alone intervention or as a key part of a comprehensive prevention program. Prevention encompasses both wellness and risk reduction. Preventive groups may focus on the reduction in the occurrence of new cases of a problem, the duration and severity of incipient problems, or they may promote strengths and optimal human functioning. (Conyne & Clanton Harpine, 2010, p. 194)

Although a short program might not fulfill all of the academic needs of children who are one or more grade levels behind in reading, a 1-week intensive program such as *Camp Sharigan* can set the stage for successful tutoring and classroom instruction by changing the students' attitudes toward reading. A prevention program of this nature must help correct deficient skills and help prevent future failure.

Although this is a school-based case example, group-centered prevention can be used with any age-group and for any prevention need. The principles are the same: group process, cohesion, intrinsic motivation, and rebuilding self-efficacy through teaching necessary skills.

Case Example 3

Therapy groups are also a logical site for prevention. Therapists wish to prevent the reoccurrence of problems that placed their clients in need of therapy. Because therapy groups use different therapeutic interventions and adapt to the clients' needs, this case example focuses only on using group process.

An outpatient group was formed for persons recently released from psychiatric inpatient care. Two graduate students from a group psychotherapy course that I was teaching had been invited to teach relaxation and stress management skills to the group. The graduate students had been invited to attend a group session prior to their instruction to get acquainted with the group members; I attended as an observer.

The therapy group began with the therapist welcoming and introducing everyone. The therapist then talked individually with each client, while the remainder of the group sat waiting their turn. This was obviously an expected practice for this group. There was no interaction among group members, nor did the therapist initiate or encourage interaction. Everyone simply sat in a circle listening and waiting their turn with the therapist.

One of the primary reasons stated for the outpatient group was prevention, but this group completely violated the principles of group psychotherapy (Yalom & Leszcz, 2005) and group prevention by not incorporating group process into the therapeutic approach. When we returned to class, one of the first questions that I presented to the graduate students was how would they initiate interaction and utilize group process in their work with this group. Even if the purpose of the group is therapy, group process, interaction, and cohesion should be an essential part of the process (Yalom & Leszcz, 2005).

The graduate student plan included having everyone start on the floor with mats going through the steps for full-body relaxation. One of the graduate students would participate in relaxation, while the other student would guide everyone through the steps. At the end, the group members would talk about feeling relaxed with the graduate student who participated in the relaxation exercise starting the discussion of how it felt to relax, the students would strive to make sure that everyone interacted. The students would then move the discussion into talking about times when we are not relaxed and what makes us feel stressed. Again, the emphasis would be on interaction, helping participants share experiences, establishing trust, and acceptance. The students planned to end their session by outlining a plan for stress reduction, encouraging each group member to share how they might adapt and implement the plan in their lives.

Group Process Is Essential for Prevention_____

Group therapy is more than just sitting in a circle of chairs (Yalom & Leszcz, 2005). Group prevention is more than just imparting information. Group process must be the central focus in all prevention groups. These three case examples demonstrate how to use three different group prevention formats, psychoeducational, group centered, and therapy based, while showing how to make full use of group process, positive group cohesion, and different styles of interaction.

A group prevention program is not effective unless it uses group process. Effective use of group process includes positive and constructive cohesion and interaction. An effective prevention group should help participants increase and improve their skills and competencies to prevent dysfunctional behavior and enhance ability to function more effectively in the future. Positive group interaction and cohesion are key factors in preventing problems and enabling participants to return to real-world settings and function effectively.

5

Using Prevention Groups in Real-World Settings

In this chapter, we will look at five short learning exercises. Each exercise may be adapted for individual reflection or as a classroom activity. First, I describe a group prevention problem, and then ask how the reader would solve the stated problem. Finally, a discussion follows, giving an example of how each prevention problem could be solved and why such a solution would be effective and in keeping with group prevention theory.

The emphasis in this chapter will be on program design. Books that discuss program design for prevention groups in more detail are also available (Conyne, 2010; Royse, Thyer, Padgett, & Logan, 2006). In my previous writings, I have suggested 25 guidelines for evaluating the effectiveness of prevention groups (Clanton Harpine, 2008) and proposed a step-by-step design guide for persons who seek guidance in designing group-centered prevention programs (Clanton Harpine, 2011). This chapter assumes that readers have experience in program design and examines the program details needed for effective prevention groups rather than giving step-by-step procedures.

All of the prevention problems in this chapter, which come from real group situations, discuss an important design principle in group prevention. Learning Exercise 1 discusses how to combine the needs of two separate groups into one program. Learning Exercise 2 highlights the differences between weeklong and yearlong prevention programs. Learning Exercise 3 focuses on how training programs can be group centered and prevention oriented. Learning Exercise 4 considers the advantages and disadvantages of mentoring-style prevention programs. Learning Exercise 5 discusses the design of group prevention programs in a hospital setting.

Group Prevention Learning Exercise 1

Prevention Problem

A community center wants to provide a prevention program for families with young preschool children. The community center plans to offer a free dinner once a week for families. After dinner, parents will participate in a lecture-focused parenting class, while the children will go to the center's computer lab and work on preschool computer-based games. The community center's goal is to help parents learn parenting skills and to help the young children be more successful in kindergarten and school.

Question

Is the center's program a group prevention program? Remember our definition from Chapter 1. How would you help this community center design a more effective group prevention program? What are the advantages and disadvantages of the program you have designed? Can you reduce or eliminate any of the disadvantages to your program?

Program Design Discussion

The preschool parenting prevention program described is really two programs in one: (1) a prevention program for preschool children and (2) a prevention program for parents. But a lecture-focused program is not prevention oriented, because it does not include group interaction; nor is a computer-based program prevention oriented. A lecture-focused program will not teach parents more effective parenting skills. Parents need hands-on practice with their children in a group setting. A computer-based preschool program will also not necessarily help preschool children be better prepared for kindergarten. Computer skills are essential in today's society, but a program to help preschool children be more successful in kindergarten must include skill-building activities, classroom management, and group skills. A group prevention program designer recognizes that it is desirable to create two separate yet intertwined programs. Ideally, a parenting program should involve both the parents and the children. Therefore, as a programmer, you must create a program that allows both groups to work individually and together.

You will need at least two trained workers to conduct two separate group programs: (1) one group worker for the parenting class and (2) a second group worker for the children's group. With children, it is always best to have at least two adults in the group at all times. Safety is an important issue, and emergencies do arise, especially with young children.

Parenting programs too often resort to lecture-focused sessions where a teacher tries to teach parents about effective family communication, discipline strategies, proper attention and praise, and social skills. Unfortunately, parents cannot learn to communicate more effectively by listening to a lecture. They cannot learn how to discipline their children by watching a video. Effective parenting classes should be hands-on and include working with real problems being experienced in the family. Generalized discussions will not transfer to actual change and prevention within a struggling family.

As a group prevention program designer, you might want to create a group-centered parenting class. Since the families meet for dinner, you might video-tape the group as they arrive and during the dinner session. Typical behavior patterns and problems are usually displayed while waiting for dinner to be served or after eating and waiting for group sessions to begin. Through vide-otapes of the actual families, you can work on real family problems rather than role plays or case examples. With such an approach, you must be careful not to embarrass families. Do not point out specific incidents or mistakes. Start by talking about problems common to all families—getting children to sit down and eat politely at the dinner table. If your discussion-focused group is positive, supportive, and becoming more cohesive with each session, then parents will begin to feel comfortable enough in the group to raise issues and problems of a more sensitive nature. Keep parenting classes discussion focused. Have specific skills that you want to teach each week and give parents an assignment. At some point in your program, parents and children should work together to practice parenting skills. Assignments might include making up a menu or a shopping list for the week, picking up toys and cleaning up together, decision making or planning a family activity, problem solving or resolving a problem that has arisen in the family, or negotiating bedtime rules and TV time. Make your assignments fit the needs of your parents. After several group sessions, you might videotape dinner time again to show improvement. Be sure to point out how parents are using the group skills that you are teaching. Encourage parents to talk about changes and improvement at home.

A discussion-focused group will enable you to teach the parenting skills in a more relevant hands-on approach. Practice time will allow parents an opportunity to apply what they are learning and give you a follow-up opportunity to work more directly with each individual family. Make your group a safe, acceptable environment in which parents feel comfortable disclosing their problems and concerns. The group leader leading such a discussion-focused parenting class must be trained in group process and prevention counseling techniques.

Even though a well-functioning family is an important component for children's success in school, children also need classroom and academic skill building to be successful in kindergarten. Computer skills, although good, are not enough. The children's session should be more than babysitting or play-time. Although learning to play cooperatively in a group is important, children need to practice classroom management. Children need hands-on activities similar to those they will experience in school classrooms. Letter awareness, phonics training, and listening skills should all be taught to help children get off to a good start in kindergarten.

A hands-on group-centered prevention approach will enable parents and children to learn the skills needed to be successful and prevent failure both as a family and as a student. Skill building is essential in both parenting and preschool programs. Without skill building, there will be no change and consequently no prevention.

This program's advantages can include lifelong improvement and mental well-being, particularly if we are able to help children and families in their early stages of development. The preschool years constitute a very important time in a family's life. Improved parenting skills and academic classroom skills are definitely prevention focused.

The disadvantages of this type of program are cost for trained staff to run the program, food cost for dinner, and a meeting space that will allow for separate group meetings and also combined group activities. Other aspects of this type of program can be the curriculum used with the children and the training activities used with the parents. Training sessions must be interactive. All class activities should be hands-on and group centered—no worksheets or memorized lists for children. Both parents and children need to develop their self-efficacy (belief that they can perform a task and be successful), and this can only be done through effective skill building. Therefore, the group approach used in both parental and children's classes becomes critical to the success of this program.

Group Prevention Learning Exercise 2

Prevention Problem

A local school wants to organize an after-school program for children who are presently failing in reading. The school has purchased a weeklong evidence-based program that cites research demonstrating its success with at-risk children. The school, however, wants to turn it into a yearlong after-school program. One of the teachers has agreed to undertake the conversion to a yearlong after-school program. The teacher is excited and says that she has lots of ideas. The school publicizes the program to parents and the community using the original name of the evidence-based weeklong program, quoting research data from the original study.

Question

What is wrong with the school's plan? How would you help this school plan an effective after-school group prevention program? Don't forget the definition of group prevention from Chapter 1 or the warnings for adapting programs listed in Chapter 3. What are the advantages and disadvantages of the after-school program you have suggested? Can you reduce or eliminate any of the disadvantages to your program?

Program Design Discussion

One of the biggest problems in group prevention is the lack of quality programming. Many schools and community organizations purchase evidence-based programs in hopes of ensuring program quality; yet as discussed in Chapter 3, the mere act of buying an evidence-based program does not guarantee evidence-based implementation. As in our example, many schools or organizations purchase a program that is shown through research to be successful. Then, the schools or organizations rewrite, change, and, in many cases, totally distort the original intent and design of the program they purchased. Therefore, the results that the school or organization receives from their redesigned version of the purchased evidence-based program are less than the original program promised. Who receives the blame? Often, the original evidence-based program is blamed for the failure of the school or organization's redesigned efforts. Rarely if ever does a school or organization admit that their redesign or implementation of the purchased program is actually the reason for program failure.

A perfect example of redesign and implementation failure comes from the "open classroom" concept of the 1960s and 1970s. The original "open classroom" concept referred to curriculum and ways to reduce the tendency of teachers to lecture in the classroom. The idea was to use learning centers and hands-on learning techniques in the classroom. The original "open classroom" concept was distorted and redesigned into a school building construction concept where schools were built without walls and without doors. Absolutely nowhere in the *original* "open classroom" concept was it ever suggested that schools should be built without walls or without doors. The original idea was to reduce the barriers within a classroom to make learning more interactive and hands-on. Yet schools used the original "open classroom" label for their distorted and redesigned construction projects. Therefore, the original "open classroom" label became known as a plan to redesign school buildings without walls rather than a hands-on curriculum. The original "open classroom" concept is to this day said to be a failure because, obviously, building schools without walls or doors is ludicrous.

Design distortion and inaccurate implementation of evidence-based programs is one of the biggest hurdles to overcome in group prevention. If we cannot maintain accuracy in the implementation of evidence-based prevention programs, then we cannot improve the effectiveness of group prevention. This is a serious problem in schools because schools provide the majority of prevention programming with children and teenagers (Kulic et al., 2004). Schools are also normally required to use evidence-based programs; however, few schools use the evidence-based programs as written. Most school personnel implementing and, in many cases, redesigning the evidence-based program do not have training in group process, interactive programming techniques, motivation, prevention program design, or facilitating a group prevention program.

Such is the case with the problem presented in this example. A trained program designer would know that you simply cannot take a weeklong group prevention program, change a few things, and redesign it into a year-long after-school program. The motivational strategies, interaction initiators, and cohesion-building techniques (all essential for an effective prevention group) are completely different for a weeklong program than they are for a yearlong program, even if both programs concern the same topic. A weeklong program is intensive but short term, and the goals of an intensive short-term group prevention program differ from the goals of a yearlong, more comprehensive program. You cannot simply change a few things, write a few new sessions, slap on the original program's label, and pretend that you have followed the original intent and design of the evidence-based program. The distorted redesign of evidence-based programs and the ineffective implementation of such programs will lead to failure.

As a group prevention program designer, you might first help this school by aiding school personnel to understand the difference between using a purchased evidence-based program as designed and changing the original design of the program. Second, you need to offer program design workshops, in-service training sessions, or conferences on how to design group prevention programs. You may also provide resources for school personnel, which provide step-by-step directions for designing school-based group prevention programs. For example, I offer a three-book series on designing group-centered prevention programs in school-based mental health. Book 1 teaches how to design an hour-long group-centered intervention (Clanton Harpine, 2008), Book 2 takes the reader step-by-step through the process of designing a weeklong intensive group-centered prevention program (Clanton Harpine, 2011), and Book 3 gives the step-by-step details for designing a group-centered yearlong after-school program (Clanton Harpine, manuscript in preparation). Why three books? Because the program design for each of these prevention programs is different. The approach for an hour-long program should differ from the approach for a weeklong program, and a yearlong program is completely different from a 1-hour or 1-week program. Different techniques, different interventions, and different motivators are needed for a 1-hour, 1-week, or yearlong program. You cannot convert a successful 1-hour intervention or even a 1-week program into a successful yearlong program by simply making a few adjustments.

Intrinsic motivation is one key to a successful yearlong program. Student motivators used in a yearlong program must be cumulative, varied, and internalized. Intrinsic motivators that work wonderfully in a weeklong program may not be enough and may not keep the motivational level high enough to keep students coming back to work over and over throughout the year.

Another key ingredient for a successful yearlong prevention program is rebuilding self-efficacy. Most schools stress self-esteem, but self-efficacy and self-esteem are not the same. Self-efficacy includes skill building (learning the skills necessary to complete a task); self-esteem is merely a feeling of self-worth. A student may be a playground bully, be failing every subject, and still display a high degree of self-esteem. A student displaying a high degree of self-efficacy on the other hand takes pride in being able to complete an academic task such as reading.

Therefore, the school in this example needs to send the staff to an effective interactive training program or purchase an evidence-based yearlong after-school program that will meet the school's needs. There is absolutely no way for school personnel, not trained in group prevention or group process, to successfully convert an evidence-based weeklong program into a yearlong after-school prevention program. You need to be more than an excellent classroom teacher with lots of creative ideas in order to design an effective yearlong after-school group prevention program. The programmer must understand group prevention program design. It truly does make a difference in program quality and actual program success and effectiveness.

The disadvantage of a call for training is that most schools do not have the funding for training programs. Well-meaning teachers with creative ideas, no matter how well intended, are not in a position to write an effective after-school yearlong group prevention program without training or help from a professional group program designer.

Hiring a trained group prevention programmer could be another alternative. The advantage of hiring a trained group prevention programmer is that once the school has developed an effective program and tested that program, they can reuse the program year after year. Again, cost will be a deterrent.

_____Group Prevention Learning Exercise 3

Prevention Problem

Local college graduates are having trouble finding jobs. The career center is planning a 3-week training program to help graduates find a job. The goal is to prevent graduates from becoming discouraged and having to accept short-term job placement rather than long-term career-oriented jobs. The career center plans to have personnel directors come and talk to the group about resume writing and cover letters, what to wear for an interview, and how to search for a job in your career field. Each weekly session will be 1-hour in length. Time will be allowed each week for questions on topics being discussed.

Question

Is this a group prevention program? Remember our definition from Chapter 1. How can a career training program become a prevention program? What would be the advantages and disadvantages of a group prevention–style training program? How would you help this career center design a more effective group prevention program? What are the advantages and disadvantages of the program you have designed? Can you reduce or eliminate any of the disadvantages to your program?

Program Design Discussion

The prevention program being planned by this career center exemplifies one of the biggest pitfalls of prevention groups: the belief that the need to impart information can only be carried out through lecture or direct teaching methods. Yes, it really is possible to teach someone how to write a resume using group-centered methods, and a group approach can even be superior to an individual one-on-one job counseling session because the group can provide motivation. The group becomes a supportive atmosphere for training and an arena in which all participants are striving to learn.

Many job placement and career center teachers complain that recent graduates and even unemployed job seekers do not believe them when they tell those seeking employment how to dress for an interview, write a cover letter, or how to prepare a resume. As one career center employee explained, "They simply think that they know more than I do; they will not listen to or take any of my advice. Talking to them is a waste of time." Sometimes a group session can be the best teacher. If the career center's goals, as listed in the program description above, are to prevent job seekers from failing in their endeavor to find career employment, then a group-centered prevention training program could be the most effective prevention approach for this group.

Using the career center's original plan of a 3-week program, the center could offer three 1-hour prevention training sessions. The center might use the following advertisement for their program:

> Would you like help getting a job? Would you like the opportunity to practice interviewing with an actual personnel director? Would you like to see your resume move to the top of the stack? All this and more awaits you at the career center's free job interviewing workshop. Call to register; space is limited.

When prospective participants call to register, they would be told to come prepared on the first night for a mock speed-interviewing session with a personnel director for a job in their career field. They would be instructed to bring a copy of a typical cover letter that they would use for a job and a copy of their resume.

Those registering for the workshop would be divided into groups according to types of jobs being sought. Personnel directors willing to conduct the mock speed-interviewing sessions would be scheduled for the first night. Each registered participant would have a 3-minute interview with a personnel director.

On arrival, each participant would be given a practice application to complete, while waiting for his or her interview number to be called. Many personnel directors say that applicants fail to get interviews because they do not know how to fill out a job application correctly. Therefore, Step 1 would be to practice filling out a job application. Learning center assistance would be provided and a station would be set up to check applications for completeness.

The personnel directors conducting the mock interviews would have a form on which they would check boxes with yes or no answers:

Would you hire this person?

Is this person dressed appropriately for an interview?

Is this person's resume up to the standard you expect?

Does this person's cover letter encourage you to want to call them for an interview?

Would you place this resume at the top of the consideration stack?

After each 3-minute interview, participants would be directed to tables with learning center directions for rewriting resumes, writing cover letters, planning interview wardrobes, looking for a job, and filling out a job application. Each participant would go to the learning center(s) for which they received an unsatisfactory checkmark at their mock interview. Each learning center would have step-by-step directions to help participants rewrite cover letters, resumes, and/or learn to fill out applications correctly. Materials and supplies would be available to enable participants to sit down and rewrite on the spot. Career center employees could be stationed at each of these learning centers to help participants.

At the close of the hour for the first session, participants would be sent home with handouts from the learning centers and an assignment to rewrite/retype cover letter, resume, or application as needed. At the second session, learning center stations would again be set up ready to help those who need help, but this time, they would be circling mistakes on resumes, applications, and cover letters that had not been corrected. Participants would move from learning center to learning center and work in small groups with others rewriting resumes and cover letters. Step-by-step directions for rewriting resumes and cover letters would again be posted at each learning center station. Helpers would provide hands-on advice for correcting and rewriting. At the second session, computer stations would also be available for help in searching for a real job and for filling out online applications. Staff would help participants learn how and where to search for job openings in their field.

At the third and final session, participants would be told to come dressed for a mock job fair. Again, personnel directors would hold mock interviews as they would at a job fair: this time, telling whether the participant would be likely to be called for a job interview or not and briefly explaining why. Participants would then go to learning center stations to correct problems that remain.

Such a 3-week workshop might be followed with an actual job fair by the career center to give participants an opportunity to demonstrate their new skills. A job fair would enable the career center to strengthen prevention efforts by encouraging participants to apply new skills learned.

Often the concept of working with others in small groups who are also engaged in the process of learning to write better resumes and cover letters is helpful to those seeking employment. Using actual skill-building sessions rather than lecture sessions gives participants the actual skills needed to improve and thereby prevent failure. Working with others who are also struggling to improve their job-hunting skills in a small and large group setting is reassuring and motivating to those who have become discouraged. Skill building is essential if you want to prevent failure. No matter how stimulating or motivating a speech may be, if someone seeking a job does not know how to write a better resume (the skills), then even the most motivating of speeches will not prevent failure. Effective prevention programs must include skill-building sessions. Effective prevention must not only impart information but also teach skills if prevention is to be effective.

One of the problems of this type of program proposal is the time needed for organizing such a program—contacting personnel directors, setting up learning centers, gathering materials, and registering participants. Yet if your goal is actually prevention, this type of program can help you provide effective training that will enable those seeking employment to be more successful.

A benefit of this type of program is that once you have organized the learning centers, they can be reused any number of times at multiple locations. Therefore, a career center could offer such a 3-week workshop multiple times with limited prep time. The learning centers would stay the same, staff would be teaching the same skills, participants would vary, and different personnel directors might need to be contacted depending on the types of jobs being sought. If you are unable to secure actual personnel directors for mock interviews, you may also ask retired career people in the fields for which participants are seeking employment. Someone who has worked in a career field can offer valuable advice.

The main advantage, though, is still the group effect. Learning as a group encourages reluctant job seekers to strive harder. If a reluctant job seeker is just sitting and listening to a speech, it is easy to get up, go home after the speech, and do nothing. If everyone is working at hands-on learning centers, it is much harder to refuse to try. If skill building is being taught, and if the program gives participants the motivation to change, then improvement is likely to result, and participants can find the pathway to being more successful.

Group Prevention Learning Exercise 4 _____

Prevention Problem

A local community counseling center is organizing a married couple's program. The counseling center is very short on funds; therefore, instead of hiring counselors, the center plans to solicit and train couples to work as mentors for discussion groups for married couples. The mentoring couple will start each discussion session by telling a short story from their own experience on a topic common to most marriages. The couple will then encourage discussion among the couples attending the session. No counselor is assigned for these group sessions nor is a specific curriculum used. The program's goal is to help married couples discuss their problems more openly in order to prevent marital difficulties and divorce. The counseling center believes that having a mentoring couple in charge of each discussion group will set a good example for the couples attending the sessions.

Question

Is this a group prevention program? Remember our definition from Chapter 1. What are the advantages and disadvantages of using trained mentoring couples? How would you help this counseling center, taking into consideration the lack of funding to design a more effective group prevention program? What are the advantages and disadvantages of the program you have designed? Can you reduce or eliminate any of the disadvantages to your program?

Program Design Discussion

In answer to the first question: Is this a prevention group? The answer could be "yes" or "no." The answer will depend entirely on how the mentoring couple facilitates the group. If the mentoring couple spends the majority of group time telling about their own experiences, such a story fulfills the same purpose as a lecture—thus, there would be no group interaction. If, however, the mentoring couple uses a quick example to initiate group interaction, then the couples group may have potential to become a prevention group.

One of the big risks with using mentoring couples is that they may lack the training and skills to handle interactive situations or problems that may arise between the couples. Mentoring couples may also not have the training to help participants learn new skills in decision making or problem solving. Any time you use mentors in a prevention group, the mentors will only be as capable as your training program trains them to be. Therefore, the critical issues in this group situation lie with selection of mentors and the training program being used with the mentoring couples. If the training program is weak or ineffective, then the couples groups will not be successful. As you plan, ask yourself the following:

What kind of training will you be offering mentoring couples?

Do you offer follow-up training?

Do you plan to ever observe the actual mentor-led group sessions?

Do you have a curriculum or plan for the groups to follow?

These become important questions because you can't simply plant a mentoring couple into a group and expect success. Mentoring can be a successful group intervention or it can be a disaster.

Mentoring programs are often the only option for community-based organizations that lack the funds to hire trained personnel. A mentoring program in and of itself is not a bad idea. The success or failure of a mentoring program lies with how the mentoring prevention groups are organized and the kind of training provided for mentors.

Selection of mentoring couples becomes a key issue with mentoring programs. If you simply accept anyone who volunteers, you may find yourself with mentoring couples who are not well suited to facilitate a cohesive interactive group discussion. One point of warning, you cannot send forth an open call for mentoring couples and then pick and choose whom you want. It is always much better to select mentoring couples because this allows you to exercise control over the couples who will facilitate your program. You may wish to use an open community-wide call for participants in the groups, but it is always better to select the group leaders or mentors.

Cohesion is essential for a mentoring group. If the mentoring group is not cohesive, it will not be successful. Remember from Chapter 2 that cohesion is not synonymous with conformity. Cohesion means that each and every group participant feels free to speak and express their ideas, feelings, and fears. This is particularly important for a couples group. If you are selecting mentoring couples, you must select couples who can generate cohesive group interaction.

Therefore, one suggestion as a prevention program designer that you might make is to start with a short-term free group-centered couples group, similar to our case example in Chapter 4. This would enable a community-based organization that finds itself lacking funds to select a strong group of mentors. Have this group led by a trained counselor. Select mentoring couples from this short-term communication for married couples group program. Such a selection process allows the counselor to see how mentoring couples function in a group setting before inviting them to become mentors. Such a selection process also allows mentoring couples to participate in a couples group before attempting to lead one. The counselor may need to conduct several couples groups before finding the adequate number of mentoring couples needed for a community-wide program. The effort is worth the search, and this type of selection process can be conducted by a single group counselor with limited funds. The benefit for prevention will be a stronger mentoring team, which becomes a key component for the success of any mentoring program.

Once the mentoring couples are selected, the group counselor must organize training sessions. Training should also be group centered and interactive.

There is also a need for follow-up training. Problems will arise. Mentors need to meet regularly to discuss and learn ways to handle problems. One suggestion is to have an ongoing mentors group, which meets with the counselor on a weekly or monthly schedule. Again, use group process.

Observations are recommended. The counselor should visit the mentoring groups periodically. This provides a stronger base for training and allows one single counselor to work with multiple groups. The counselor should not take over the group from the mentoring couple but, instead, provide support. Observations can also be helpful in follow-up training. The counselor might say, "I can see exactly what you were talking about last week when I visited your group, your group members really do. . . ." The counselor could then help all of the mentors learn how to deal with the problem through a non-threatening interactive group training approach.

The counselor may also wish to develop a curriculum or discussion schedule for the groups to follow. Any curriculum used must be interactive for groups to be successful. So be careful in selecting a group curriculum.

One word of caution, if the group counselor organizing this mentoring program is not well trained in group process and prevention and does not conduct interactive group sessions, the mentoring program is doomed before it starts. You cannot teach what you do not understand or practice. Therefore, a group counselor attempting to organize such a program as described must be able to lead a cohesive, interactive prevention group as well as train others to do so in order for this mentoring program to be successful. You cannot learn how to facilitate an interactive, cohesive prevention group by simply reading a textbook. The counselor and mentors should have actual hands-on group training.

One of the disadvantages of this type of approach is time. It takes more time to organize a mentoring program using selection, training, and follow-up, but the results are worth the time invested.

_____Group Prevention Learning Exercise 5

Prevention Problem

A hospital is organizing a group prevention program for patients who have suffered heart attacks. The hospital plans to bring in doctors, nurses who work with heart patients, patients who successfully recovered from a heart attack, and an exercise coordinator. The heart attack patients will participate in an hour-long exercise program before the group session. The plan is to have group sessions immediately following exercise. Each speaker will talk for 20 minutes, and then allow questions from the group. Each group session is planned for 50 minutes.

Question

Is the hospital's plan a group prevention program? Remember our definition from Chapter 1. How would you help this hospital design a more effective group prevention program? What are the advantages and disadvantages of the program you have designed? Can you reduce or eliminate any of the disadvantages to your program?

Program Design Discussion

In answer to the first question, "Is this hospital-based group a prevention group?" The answer is "no." The hospital is planning an hour of exercise, 20 minutes of lecture, and a 30-minute question and answer period. Asking and answering questions is not group interaction. For a group to be interactive, the group members must work, talk, and interact with one another as well as the group leader. Exercise can be either individual or group oriented. Most group exercise programs are leader directed. Therefore, this group prevention plan lacks one of the primary requirements listed in our definition in Chapter 1. It does not include group interaction. The first thing needed in redesigning this program is an interactive format. This group for heart attack patients is a group that must provide mutual support from group members to be successful. If the group participants do not think that other group members care about them and support them in their efforts to make these difficult lifestyle changes, the prevention program will not be successful. Care and cohesive support can only be established through an interactive group. Passive participation does not generate support and acceptance.

Let us turn next to the needs of the patients participating in this program. Most patients after a heart attack face the difficulty of making major lifestyle changes: exercise, diet, reducing stress, stop smoking or drinking alcohol, sometimes even career changes. Motivation is one of the key factors in helping people make these lifestyle changes. Fear can be a strong motivational initiator, but fear does not usually motivate people to change over a long period of time. Fear works for short-term change. A doctor may tell a patient "if you do not change your lifestyle, the next heart attack could kill you." The heart attack patient may be motivated out of fear to attend an exercise program, lose weight, and change eating habits, even stop smoking or drinking alcohol for a short period of time. Unfortunately, if fear is your only motivator or your primary motivator, your program to prevent future heart attacks will be unsuccessful. As the primary motivator for change, fear cannot be sustained over a long period of time. The heart attack patient needs intrinsic (internal) motivation. Intrinsic motivators can help heart attack patients make permanent lifestyle changes. Any prevention program that you design must include intrinsic motivation.

Prevention groups also need a positive, supportive cohesive atmosphere. This is true for all prevention groups but especially a group in which heart attack patients are being asked to make permanent major lifestyle changes.

Many hospitals organize prevention groups for heart attack patients. Some groups are successful, some are not. Continued long-term attendance is a stated problem with such groups. Heart attack patients often start with a degree of dedication but fizzle over time in attendance and commitment. How will your program generate long-term commitment? Cohesion is one of the keys to commitment. People are more likely to continue participating in a group in which they feel accepted and in a group that they feel is helping to bring about desired and needed changes. This is why, in many hospital-based heart attack patient prevention groups, patients attend the exercise portion of the program but find excuses not to attend the lecture-based portion of the prevention program. Lectures do not create a cohesive group atmosphere.

So as a group prevention program designer, what advice can you offer this hospital? A more action-oriented hands-on approach could definitely be one suggestion. Create a 2-hour program that meets three times a week. Each session would begin with a basic health check from a nurse on weight, blood pressure, and pulse. Patients would also be encouraged to state any problems or concerns they are having to the nurse. The hour-long exercise session would include an individual exercise program developed with an exercise specialist to meet each patient's individual exercise needs. Each exercise session would end with a group exercise that everyone could participate with; a group exercise would naturally need to be selected to match the capabilities of the specific group members. A group exercise would also help participants work together as a supportive group.

Exercise time would transition right into relaxation training. Instead of having a break between exercise time and group time, relaxation exercises would allow participants to learn how to reduce stress and also make the transition from exercise time to group time. For example, relaxation should not only be taught lying on exercise mats on the floor but also in chairs so that participants who are returning to the workplace may learn relaxation exercises that they can use while sitting at a desk or in a chair.

Relaxation exercises should be followed with an active hands-on group activity to build group interaction and cohesion. Such group activities could include making and eating a healthy snack, food tasting with recipes and cooking tips, shopping for healthy food items, or evaluating restaurant menus in small groups to determine which entrées would be healthier. Hands-on activities could help initiate and lead into group-centered discussions about the problems of maintaining a healthy diet, making healthy food choices, or planning healthy menus. These should be group-centered discussions, not lectures. The group could even plan dinner parties with healthy menus at member homes or go to a restaurant together once a month and stress eating a healthy meal.

Candid and supportive discussions on healthy eating can pave the way for disclosure by group members on other lifestyle change–related problems. A trained group counselor could help group members share and work on lifestyle changes. For example, if the group includes several participants who must stop smoking as part of their health plan, then discussions might include step-by-step assistance and group support in ceasing to smoke. If losing weight is a major problem for group participants, then support and plans may be offered to help them lose weight. The focus would be on group discussion and learning through group discussion. The group would become a positive, supportive peer group that would help group members tackle and carry out lifestyle changes.

What are the advantages of a program like this? One of the first and foremost advantages of an interactive prevention program is that it creates a supportive atmosphere in which cohesion can grow and be maintained. It is easier to make major lifestyle changes and to maintain those changes long term if you are a member of a supportive group in which others are also struggling to make lifestyle changes. Incorporating hands-on learning, such as making healthy snacks or planning healthy menus and meals, allows group participants to learn not only new ideas but also new skills.

Motivation is an essential component of this program. It will be important to chart and show improvement week to week. Motivation must be intrinsic. Another key component for a prevention program for heart attack patients is that the program must take individual needs into account, and the fears and personalities of each participant must be considered. You cannot simply plan a generic program. The program must meet the specific needs of the individual participants.

One of the disadvantages of this type of program is cost. The program plan calls for a nurse, exercise specialist, a group counselor to facilitate group discussions, and, possibly, even a nutritionist. The group counselor must be skilled in interactive group techniques. While hospitals may be able to assign staff, interns, or even students to some of these jobs to save cost, a cohesive interactive group structure is essential for the success of this program. Training in group skills is often lacking. Additional group training may be required for personnel to facilitate an interactive group structure. While cost is a factor, prevention is cheaper than treatment.

The Future of Prevention Group Programming _____

Group interaction and cohesion are essential for the success of any prevention group. Skill building is essential for change. Training in group process and prevention techniques must be increased. If group prevention is to grow and endure, we must enact change.

For example, schools are the major source of mental health services for children (Brown & Tracy, 2008), with 70% of children's counseling groups occurring in schools (Hoag & Burlingame, 1997), and with prevention being one of the primary foci of school counseling (Kulic et al., 2004), it is natural that we would look for new and different approaches to meet the needs of children and teens in school-based settings. When we factor in recent surveys that show that prevention techniques are becoming less common in counseling (Goodyear et al., 2008), the need to increase group prevention in school-based settings becomes alarmingly clear. The problem seems more striking if we include research that demonstrates that schools that offer group prevention programs show stronger academic achievement, have a lower dropout rate, even have fewer absentee problems, and are less likely to have bullying, teasing, fighting, or behavior issues (Adelman & Taylor, 2006; Buhs, Ladd, & Herald, 2006).

The need to increase and improve group prevention in school-based settings is evident. Groups provide the best prevention approach in schools (Slavin, 2002), but prevention groups, to be effective, must make sure that all students work together in the group as equals (Marmarosh & Markin, 2007).

Most prevention programs offered in the schools use a psychoeducational format. While there are many excellent school-based psychoeducational group prevention programs (Horne, Stoddard, & Bell, 2007), there are also many programs in school-based settings using the psychoeducational or group prevention label but which do not adhere to the group process structure and standards of group prevention as outlined in Chapter 1.

Cohesion is essential in group prevention, and cohesion can only occur if every single group member is accepted as an equal participant (Marmarosh et al., 2005). Lectures do not create cohesive prevention groups. Many groups are attaching a prevention label to lectures and classifying such a session as counseling or group prevention. This must stop. We need to find ways to help everyone working in prevention to use group prevention correctly.

References _____

Ablon, J., & Jones, E. (2002). Validity of controlled clinical trials of psychotherapy: Findings from the NIMH treatment of depression collaborative research program. *American Journal of Psychiatry, 159,* 775–783.

Adelman, H. S., & Taylor, L. (2006). Mental health in schools and public health. *Public Health Report, 121,* 294–298.

Bandura, A. (1977). Self-efficacy: Toward a unifying theory of behavioral change. *Psychological Review, 84,* 191–215.

Bandura, A. (1997). *Self-efficacy: The exercise of control.* New York, NY: W. H. Freeman.

Baumeister, R. F., & Leary, M. R. (1995). The need to belong: Desire for interpersonal attachments as a fundamental human motivation. *Psychological Review, 103,* 5–33.

Biglan, A., Mrazek, P., Carnine, D., & Flay, B. R. (2003). The integration of research and practice in the prevention of youth problem behaviors. *American Psychologist, 58,* 433–440. doi:10.1037/0003-066X.58.6-7.433

Brigman, G., & Webb, L. (2007). Student success skills: Impacting achievement through large and small group work. *Group Dynamics: Theory, Research, and Practice, 11,* 283–292. doi:10.1037/1089-2699.11.4.283

Brown, S., & Tracy, E. M. (2008). Building communities of practice to advance mental health services in schools. *The Community Psychologist, 41,* 46–49.

Buhs, E. S., Ladd, G. W., & Herald, S. (2006). Peer exclusion and victimization: Processes that mediate the relation between peer group rejection and children's classroom engagement and achievement? *Journal of Educational Psychology, 98,* 1–13. doi:10.1037/0022-0663.98.1.1

Catalano, R. F., Mazza, J. J., Harachi, T. W., Abbott, R. D., Haggerty, K. P., & Fleming, C. B. (2003). Raising healthy children through enhancing social development in elementary school: Results after 1.5 years. *Journal of School Psychology, 41,* 143–164.

Clanton Harpine, E. (2005, August). After-school community-based prevention project. In Carl Paternite (Chair), *Using community science to promote school-based mental health.* Symposium conducted at the annual convention of the American Psychological Association, Washington, DC.

Clanton Harpine, E. (2007, August). *A community-based after-school prevention program: A one year review of the Camp Sharigan Program.* Paper presented at the annual convention of the American Psychological Association, San Francisco, CA.

Clanton Harpine, E. (2008). *Group interventions in schools: Promoting mental health for at-risk children and youth.* New York, NY: Springer.

Clanton Harpine, E. (2010). *Erasing failure in the classroom: Vol. 1. Camp Sharigan, a ready-to-use group-centered intervention for grades 1-3* (2nd ed.). Aiken, SC: Group-Centered Learning.

Clanton Harpine, E. (2011). *Group-centered prevention programs for at-risk students.* New York, NY: Springer.

Clanton Harpine, E. (in press). *After-school prevention programs for at-risk students.* New York, NY: Springer.

Clanton Harpine, E., Nitza, A., & Conyne, R. (2010). Prevention groups: Today and tomorrow. *Group Dynamics: Theory, Research, and Practice, 14,* 268–280. doi:10.1037/a0020579

Clanton Harpine, E., & Reid, T. (2009). Enhancing academic achievement in a Hispanic immigrant community: The role of reading in academic failure and mental health. *School Mental Health, 1,* 159–170. doi:10.1007/s12310-009-9011-z

Conyne, R. K. (2004). *Preventive counseling: Helping people to become empowered in systems and settings.* New York, NY: Brunner-Routledge.

Conyne, R. K. (2010). *Preventive program development and evaluation: An incidence reduction, culturally relevant approach.* Thousand Oaks, CA: Sage.

Conyne, R. K., & Clanton Harpine, E. (2010). Prevention groups: The shape of things to come. *Group Dynamics: Theory, Research, and Practice, 14,* 193–198. doi:10.1037/a0020446

Davis, J. B. (1914). *Vocational and moral guidance.* Boston, MA: Ginn.

Deci, E. L., & Ryan, R. M. (1985). *Intrinsic motivation and self-determination in human behavior.* New York, NY: Plenum Press.

Durlak, J. A., & Wells, A. M. (1997). Primary prevention mental health programs for children and adolescents: A meta-analytic review. *American Journal of Community Psychology, 25,* 115–152.

Finn, J. D., Gerber, S. B., & Boyd-Zaharias, J. (2005). Small classes in the early grades, academic achievement, and graduating from high school. *Journal of Educational Psychology, 97,* 214–223.

Fuhriman, A., & Burlingame, G. M. (1990). Consistency of matter: A comparative analysis of individual and group process variables. *The Counseling Psychologist, 18,* 6–63.

Gazda, G. M., Ginter, E. J., & Horne, A. M. (2001). *Group counseling and group psychotherapy: Theory and application.* Boston, MA: Allyn & Bacon.

Goodyear, R. K., Murdock, N., Lichtenberg, J. W., McPherson, R., Koetting, K., & Petren, S. (2008). Stability and change in counseling psychologists' identities, roles, functions, and career satisfaction across 15 years. *The Counseling Psychologist, 36,* 220–249.

Greenberg, M., Domitrovich, C., & Bumbarger, B. (2001). The prevention of mental disorders in school-aged children: Current state of the field. *Prevention and Treatment, 4,* 1–48. Retrieved from http://journals.apa.org/prevention/volume 4/pre0040001a.html

Greenberg, M., Weissberg, R. P., O'Brien, M. U., Zins, J. E., Fredricks, L., Resnick, H., & Elias, M. J. (2003). Enhancing school-based prevention and youth development through coordinated social, emotional, and academic learning. *American Psychologist, 58,* 466–474. doi:10.1037/0003-066X.58.6-7.466

Greene, J. P., & Winters, M. (2006). *Leaving boys behind: Public high school graduation rates*. New York, NY: Manhattan Institute for Policy Research.

Hage, S. M., & Romano, J. L. (2010). History of prevention and prevention groups: Legacy for the 21st century. *Group Dynamics: Theory, Research, and Practice, 14,* 199–210. doi:10.1037/a0020736

Hoag, M. A., & Burlingame, G. M. (1997). Evaluating the effectiveness of child and adolescent group treatment: A meta-analytic review. *Journal of Clinical Child Psychology, 26,* 234–246.

Hogg, M. A., Abrams, D., Otten, S., & Hinkle, S. (2004). The social identity perspective: Intergroup relations, self-conception, and small groups. *Small Group Research, 35,* 246–276.

Holmes, S. E., & Kivlighan, D. M. (2000). Comparison of therapeutic factors in group and individual treatment processes. *Journal of Counseling Psychology, 47,* 478–484.

Holtz, R. (2004). Group cohesion, attitude projection, and opinion certainty: Beyond interaction. *Group Dynamics: Theory, Research, and Practice, 8,* 112–125.

Horne, A. M., Stoddard, J. L., & Bell, C. D. (2007). Group approaches to reducing aggression and bullying in school. *Group Dynamics: Theory, Research, and Practice, 11,* 262–271. doi:10.1037/1089-2699.11.4.262

Kazak, A. E. (2008). Evidence-based treatment and practice: New opportunities to bridge clinical research and practice, enhance the knowledge base, and improve patient care. *American Psychologist, 63,* 146–159. doi:10.1037/0003-066X.63.3.146

Kazak, A. E., Hoagwood, K., Weisz, J. R., Hood, K., Kratochwill, T. R., Vargas, L. A., & Banez, G. A. (2010). A meta-systems approach to evidence-based practice for children and adolescents. *American Psychologist, 65,* 85–97. doi:10.1037/a0017784

Keller, T., A., & Just, M. A. (2009). Altering cortical connectivity: Remediation-induced changes in the white matter of poor readers. *Neuron, 64,* 624–631. doi:10.1016/j.neuron.2009.10.018

Kratochwill, T. R. (2007). Preparing psychologists for evidence-based school practice: Lessons learned and challenges ahead. *American Psychologist, 62,* 826–843.

Kulic, K. R., Horne, A. M., & Dagley, J. C. (2004). A comprehensive review of prevention groups for children and adolescents. *Group Dynamics: Theory, Research, and Practice, 8,* 139–151.

Langley, A. K., Nadeem, E., Kataoka, S. H., Stein, B. D., & Jaycox, L. H. (2010). Evidence-based mental health programs in schools: Barriers and facilitators of successful implementation. *School Mental Health, 2,* 105–113. doi:10.1007/s12310-010-9038-1

Lazell, E. W. (1921). The group treatment of dementia praecox. *Psychoanalytical Review, 8,* 168–179.

Marmarosh, C., Holtz, A., & Schottenbauer, M. (2005). Group cohesiveness, group-derived collective self-esteem, group-derived hope, and the well-being of group therapy members. *Group Dynamics: Theory Research and Practice, 9,* 32–44.

Marmarosh, C., & Markin, R. D. (2007). Group and personal attachments: Two is better than one when predicting college adjustment. *Group Dynamics: Theory Research and Practice, 11,* 153–164.

Marsh, L. C. (1931). Group treatment of the psychoses by the psychological equivalent of the revival. *Mental Hygiene in New York, 15,* 328–349.

McHugh, R. K., & Barlow, D. H. (2010). The dissemination and implementation of evidence-based psychological treatments: A review of current efforts. *American Psychologist, 65,* 73–84. doi:10.1037/a0018121

McHugh, R. K., Murray, H. W., & Barlow, D. H. (2009). Balancing fidelity and adaptation in the dissemination of empirically supported treatments: The promise of transdiagnostic interventions. *Behavior Research and Therapy, 47,* 946–953. doi:10.1016/j.brat.2009.07.005

Miller, R. L., & Shinn, M. (2005). Learning from communities: Overcoming difficulties in the dissemination of prevention and promotion efforts. *American Journal of Community Psychology, 35,* 169–183.

Nastasi, B. K., Moore, R. B., & Varjas, K. M. (2004). *School-based mental health services: Creating comprehensive and culturally specific programs.* Washington, DC: American Psychological Association.

Nation, M., Crusto, C., Wandersman, A., Kumpfer, K. L., Seybolt, D., Morrissey-Kane, E., & Davino, K. (2003). What works in prevention: Principles of effective prevention programs. *American Psychologist, 58,* 449–456. doi:10.1037/0003-066X.58.6-7.449

National Assessment of Educational Progress. (2009). *Nation's report card: Reading 2009.* Retrieved from http://nces.ed.gov/nationsreportcard/pdf/main2009/2010458.pdf

Nelson, G., Westhues, A., & MacLeod, J. (2003). A meta-analysis of longitudinal research on preschool prevention programs for children. *Prevention and Treatment, 6,* Article 0031a. Retrieved from http://journals.apa.org/prevention/volume 6/preoo60031a.html

O'Brien Caughy, M., Murray Nettles, S., & O'Campo, P. J. (2008). The effect of residential neighborhood on child behavior problems in first grade. *American Journal of Community Psychology, 42,* 39–50.

Ogrodniczuk, J. S., & Piper, W. E. (2003). The effect of group climate on outcome in two forms of short-term group therapy. *Group Dynamics: Theory Research and Practice, 7,* 64–76.

Orfield, G., & Lee, C. (2005). *Why segregation matters: Poverty and educational inequality.* Cambridge, MA: The Civil Right Project at Harvard University.

Posthuma, B. W. (2002). *Small groups in counseling and therapy: Process and leadership* (4th ed.). Boston, MA: Allyn & Bacon.

Prilleltensky, I., Nelson, G., & Pierson, L. (2001). The role of power and control in children's lives: An ecological analysis of pathways toward wellness, resilience and problems. *Journal of Community and Applied Social Psychology, 11,* 143–158.

Riggs, N. R., Bohnert, A. M., Guzman, M. D., & Davidson, D. (2010). Examining the potential of community-based after-school programs for Latino youth. *American Journal of Community Psychology, 45,* 417–429. doi:10.1007/s10464-010-9313-1

Rogers, C. (1970). *Encounter groups.* New York, NY: Harper & Row.

Royse, D., Thyer, B. A., Padgett, D. K., & Logan, T. K. (2006). *Program evaluation: An introduction* (4th ed.). Belmont, CA: Thomson Brooks/Cole.

Slavin, R. L. (2002). Operative group dynamics in school settings: Structuring to enhance educational, social, and emotional progress. *Group, 26,* 297–308.

Snowden, L. R. (2005). Racial, cultural and ethnic disparities in health and mental health: Toward theory and research at community levels. *American Journal of Community Psychology, 35,* 1–8.

Tobler, N., & Stratton, H. (1997). Effectiveness of school-based drug prevention programs: A meta-analysis of the research. *Journal of Primary Prevention, 18,* 71–128.

Twenge, J., & Campbell, W. K. (2002). Self-esteem and socioeconomic status: A meta-analytic review. *Personality and Social Psychology Review, 6,* 59–71.

Wandersman, A., & Florin, P. (2003). Community interventions and effective prevention. *American Psychologist, 58,* 441–448. doi:10.1037/0003-066X.58.6-7.441

Weissberg, R., Kumpfer, K., & Seligman, M. (2003). Prevention that works for children and youth: An introduction. *American Psychologist, 58,* 425–432. doi:10.1037/0003-066X.58.6-7.425

Yalom, I. D., & Leszcz, M. (2005). *The theory and practice of group psychotherapy* (5th ed.). New York, NY: Basic Books.

Index _____

About the Author_____

Elaine Clanton Harpine, PhD, is a motivational psychologist specializing in group-centered motivational program design. She has 40 years of experience designing and conducting motivational programs for children and youth. Dr. Clanton Harpine earned her doctorate in educational psychology, counseling from the University of Illinois, Urbana–Champaign.

Dr. Clanton Harpine has published 13 nonfiction books, including *Group-Centered Prevention Programs for At-Risk Students* (2011), *Group Interventions in Schools: Promoting Mental Health for At-Risk Children and Youth* (2008), and *No Experience Necessary!*, which received an Award of Excellence in 1995 and was selected as one of the top five children's books in its class.

Her research for the past 10 years has focused on using group-centered interventions with at-risk readers. Dr. Clanton Harpine designed the motivational reading program called *Camp Sharigan*, which she has used extensively in her work and research. She also designed the *Reading Orienteering Club* after-school program and *4-Step Method* for teaching at-risk children to read. Her research with these programs has been published in psychological journals and reported through presentations at the American Psychological Association's annual conventions.

In recent years, Dr. Clanton Harpine has been teaching group therapy and counseling, lifespan development, and human growth and development at the University of South Carolina Aiken and is continuing her research with group-centered prevention. She is the editor for the "Prevention Corner" column that appears quarterly in *The Group Psychologist*. She was selected for inclusion in *Who's Who of American Women*, 2006–2012, for her work with children in inner-city neighborhoods.

⑤SAGE research**methods**

The essential online tool for researchers from the world's leading methods publisher

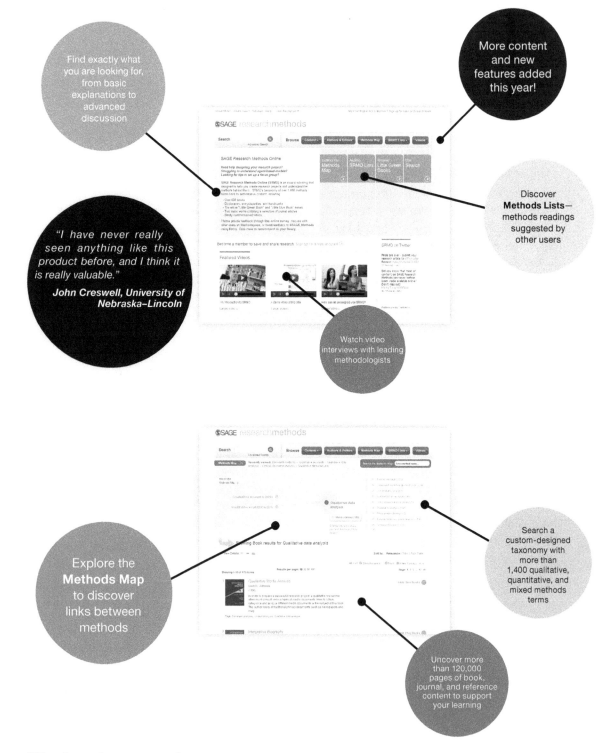

Find exactly what you are looking for, from basic explanations to advanced discussion

More content and new features added this year!

Discover **Methods Lists**— methods readings suggested by other users

"*I have never really seen anything like this product before, and I think it is really valuable.*"

John Creswell, University of Nebraska–Lincoln

Watch video interviews with leading methodologists

Explore the **Methods Map** to discover links between methods

Search a custom-designed taxonomy with more than 1,400 qualitative, quantitative, and mixed methods terms

Uncover more than 120,000 pages of book, journal, and reference content to support your learning

Find out more at
www.sageresearchmethods.com

CPSIA information can be obtained
at www.ICGtesting.com
Printed in the USA
JSHW020033250120
3793JS00002B/6